CW01149378

ache .

chloe ann

to everyone
who bugged me incessantly enough
for this to become

thank you

the ache	9
the lovers	51
the rest	95

the ache

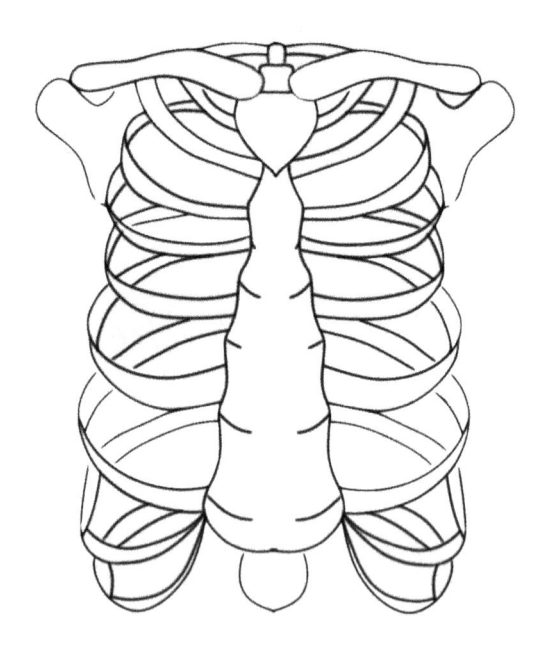

the sad settled
like a cold shadow
between the cracks
in my ribcage
leaving my heart
in a dark cave

it was never the pain
it was watching it heal
thinking that maybe one day
it would be my mind
and not my skin

i cannot
i will not
let this sadness go
it's intertwined within my soul
i am not happy
i am sad
and that's kind of it

the waves crashed against the shore
wind whipped up the sand
and carried it
the sun dipped below the horizon
the moon hid
just as i did
in the vast dunes of sand
and the drowning sound of the water
shattering the quiet night

the cold hit
and everything stopped
again

i am afraid
once i crack
i will never stop
breaking

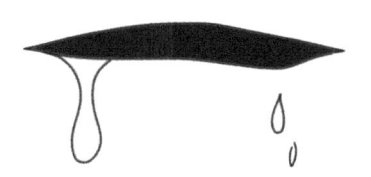

i want to be poetry and green tea
soft sweaters and vanilla
but i'm aching and rusted
jagged edges and overflowing

it's sitting in my throat
and i can't swallow it
i'm choking
i won't/can't cry for help

i want to cocoon myself
buried deep
where no one can reach me
and stay there

blue water runs beneath my skin

(freezing cold, bringing me life)

the aching hollow
swallows me up
eroding my banks
collapsing into me

everything is so vast
and i am so lost

i am six feet under, dirt suffocating my tired body.
roots pushed my ribs apart; i am their home. my
mouth fills with soil and i can't breathe

i want to pull my skin apart
to see what's inside
what runs so slowly
through my veins
threatening to stop my heart
and seep through the cracks

spiders made me their home
their threads holding me together
glinting in the light
of my ivory bones and hollow organs

and i starved myself
until i felt nothing
but it was never enough
to be nothing

how does anyone
exist
in their body
in their mind
how do they find peace?
how do they sleep at night?

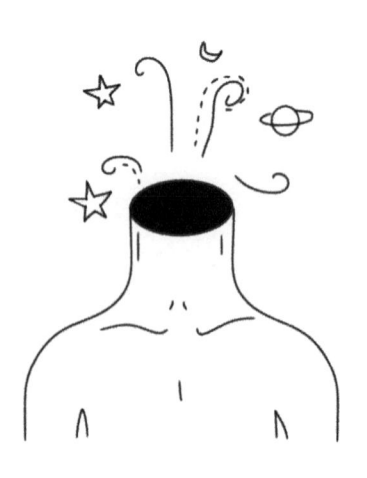

the silence of the ocean
the expanse of the universe
one distorted
comforts me

i am trying to rid myself
of these rotten pieces
how do i dispose of this body i've grown

i didn't know how i felt
all i knew was i wanted to rip this feeling
from my body
and wash my soul

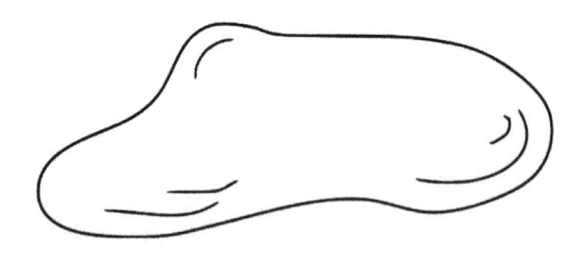

i used to run warm
my blood feeding my body
now my blood is outside
staining my skin red
crusted
i can't get it off

and it's time
to rip this flesh from my bones
for i do not need this space
to occupy i do not deserve
let me starve myself
into oblivion

2am is my vice
keeping me sane
the lack of sleep
hurts
but the silence of the night
is so comforting

i am rotting
from the inside
so tell me again
what is the need
if not to continue to rot

i wrapped myself tightly
in thorns and weeds
piercing my skin to the bone
red waterfalls from my flesh
pooling beneath my feet
and to the sky i screamed

is this what it is like to be held

everything is burning around me
i might finally feel the warmth
this life was meant to bring
set me alight

my ribs creak under my skin
if i breathe too fast
they'll snap
leaking my last breath
into the stale air
of my despair

you could hear the water rushing
behind her eyes
cascading
a torrent of unsaid words
of unspoken thoughts

my throat rips
my fingers bleed
poison dripping from my lips
acid running through my veins

i bled silently
waves from an un-stitched wound
blue water running red
seeping through my skin

i cry to the stars

let me come home

water ran down her body
torrents rushing across her skin
rivers
streams
it dripped from her fingers
eroding the ground
beneath her

i buried my thoughts
and at 3am
they tear their way
out of my chest
demanding to be felt

she started running
when her banks broke
but you can't run
if you're drowning

i stood
at the edge of the cliff
looking down
toes gripping clay
wind whipping through my hair
i threw my arms back
this time
no one will save me

the lovers

you were broken glass but i stood there and watched the blood run down my fingers anyway

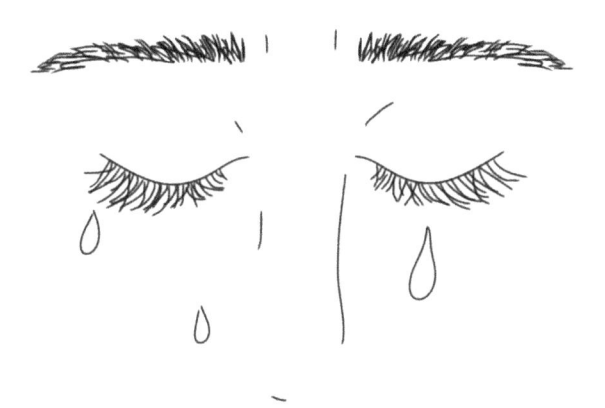

i am blue storms
and you seem to be
getting tired
of melancholy

i dreamed of you leaving
the hurt followed me
around like
an impending storm
i swallowed shards of ice
and imagined it glass
ripping my throat open
and stealing the last words
thoughts
i had of you
deep in my subconscious

i was a fucking wild fire
you let me burn
i was smouldering ashes
you smothered me
i am charred remains
and now you return
wondering what the fuck happened
to the fire i was
when you both
set me alight
and watched me burn out

don't you dare
come back into my life
telling me that
i hurt myself last time

you are not innocent

i dream of sinning when i am with you
and it terrifies me
that another person
can make me feel
what i did not know
i could
that so many have taught me
i could not
                              (i hope i do not forget myself)

i want you to fall to your knees
and worship
the way i envisioned you
as my own goddamn religion

i am too intense
burning internally
i threw myself into you
you licked the flames
and flinched
i think i burnt you

i stand here with my arms wide
my heart naked, outside my body
but you stand and watch me
give myself to you
you do not take my heart
but you do not welcome me
the irony is
i gave my heart to you long ago

i think it died

(you did not care for it)

my love
end my wars
dull my blades
i'm tired of hurting
i've given you my mind
written on squares of
thick paper
please don't leave me
let me stay

i saw everything that you were
and ignored everything that you weren't

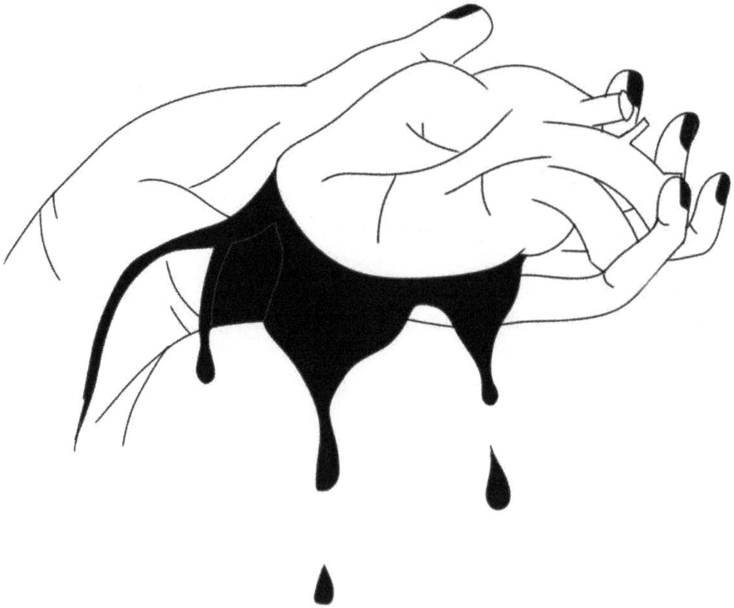

boy/dream/him
held my heart in
his dirty hands
for too long
coagulated pulse
dried out and cracked
he put it on the floor
stepped over it
guilty glances *no*
i shoved my ribs apart
begging my body to
accept the rejected love
again
the dirt of his hands
swims around my veins
my blue blood black
my heart still cold and
hard
he tried to give it back

he cannot return
what he broke

i am stubborn
but this is stale love
did you really think
i wouldn't give up?
that's on you

i shattered
crumbled piece by piece
you told me it was my fault
and there was nothing to fix

you did this to yourself

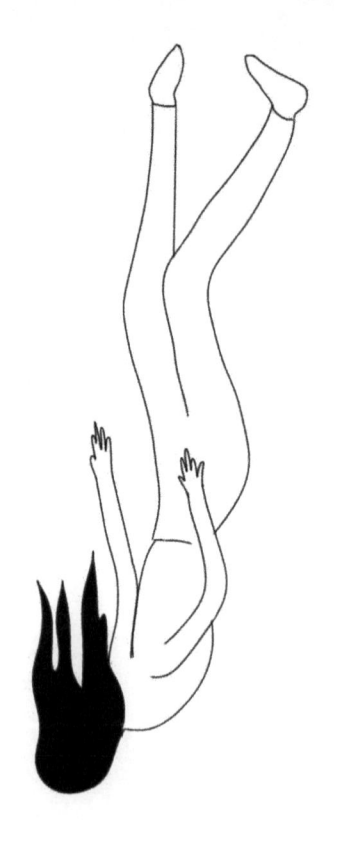

i should have told you i loved you
i waited until i was drowning
my mouth filled with water
and i swallowed your name whole
deep into my lungs

i cried
whenever i was with you
because the thing that
broke my heart
was a thought
that has never
even crossed your mind

am i beautiful without you?

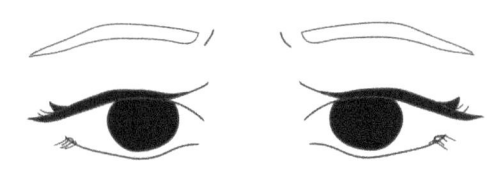

and there he was
those eyes that never saw me

the blood in my mouth
begins to taste sweet
i think i prefer the pain
over keeping you

i cannot expect
you to stay
while i am digging
my own grave

why does my heart break
every time i see you
over
and over
and over
again

the world is so big
the stars so bright
and your eyes are so sad

please let me in

the night stretches for hours more
the moon glints across the ocean
and i wonder
if you thought i was joking
when i asked/begged you to stay
stay
and you laughed
as you left

i thought i understood your longing
but perhaps i was looking in a mirror

i used to love you
i didn't when we kissed

there is something
in the silence of longing
that leaves me
aching for you

i search your eyes
for a sign
but get nothing
in return

and in an attempt to bring myself closer to you, i threw myself off bridges, drank litres of alcohol and tore myself open. i didn't heal. i drowned myself trying to stay afloat, breathing in lungfuls of salty water, pulling the life from my body. i was trying to get you to love me, but broken doesn't heal broken. it breaks the fragile worlds we build for ourselves and in the end, we both end up crying.

i guess i just want to know
who my destination is
whether or not these distractions
along the way
have been the one
and i lost them
let them go
ran away because i was afraid
or if they are still somewhere
waiting for me

your absence
brought me silence
and in the silence
i found peace

please do not come back

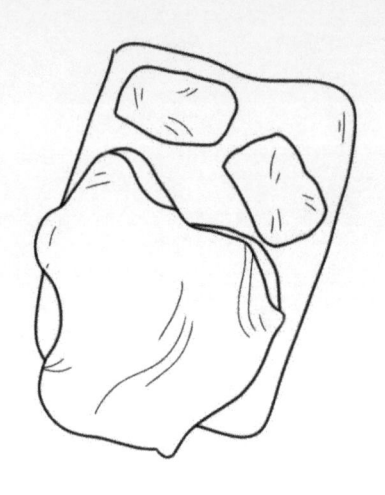

they were beside me
curled around themselves
sleeping
but facing away
for even in sleep
no one could bare
to face me

i disappeared
in the hope that
maybe you might notice
but of course
you never did

of course

i fell in love with ideas
soft spoken words and whispers
the late night texts
the laughter and side glances
it broke me
my own heart torn
and they watched from afar
i dissolved into myself
all i got in return
were guilty glances and an empty stare

do not love
when you are lonely
do not trust them
with the last piece
of your happiness

when i look at you now
i wince
my eyes flickering
a shiver down my spine
the future we never dreamed about
is now just as much of an empty thought
i mourn sometimes
for all that we could have been
and for all that we chose not to become

he must do something
about that laugh of his
i forget i have lungs
when i hear it

you shone the brightest shade of yellow, when all you should have been was red warning lights. you gave me poison and i drank it like water and still wondered why it burned a gaping hole inside me. it burned. the way the lights of an ambulance at 3am in the rear view mirror do. except this time, i told myself the burn was part of your love. maybe if i loved you more i wouldn't feel the pain of silent text messages and non answers to my longing questions. because of course it was me, it was the flaw of my love. never yours. you were always bright yellow, like the rising sun after a storm, and i should have run to the fucking ocean to drown in blue instead.

the rest

i am drenched in night
galaxies dance in my eyes
stardust surrounds me
like a halo
seeps from my pores
it's beautiful
but i am choking

i bury my sadness
beneath my skin
how else am i meant
to release it?
to remain it is poison
burning through my veins
straight to the heart

lay me down
in the softest grass
let the sunlight hit me
fill my hurt with light
leave me in the grass
i will grow flowers
and turn into something beautiful

let me make a home
out of this morbid corpse
until i bleed blue
waves cascading from my shores

let me carve myself
out of these pale bones
shrouded in darkness
ripping through my skin

let me rest this soul
sleeping between these organs
stars under my ribcage
i will be eternal

if i am to die, i want to die shouting my favourite songs, so loud my neighbours sing along. i want to die dancing around the kitchen, catching my shin on the dishwasher and leaving footprints on mums clean floor as i spin. i want to die holding your hand in the ocean, seaweed tickling our toes and making us shriek, falling into each other laughing at our fear. to die with stains on my clothes from my favourite foods, my fingers sticky, syrup running down my neck. i will not die alone. i will not die in darkness. i will be loved, and i will share it with the world

> to heal
> is to put everything
> back together
> but what if
> these pieces of me
> don't fit together?

why does healing hurt more than falling apart

is it a privilege
to be held by someone
who falls in and out of themselves
or a curse
they can only give you
what they give themselves

tell me tell me tell me
let me know
when does the ache stop
the calling out for more
for what i am not
the hollow of need
no
want
i feel like my soul
is not among the stars anymore
how do i sit comfortably
here
always here
and not long for more?
where is the end
how do i return this ache
to the stars

the sun rises continuously
light touches beautiful
so leave your curtains open
and beckon the embrace
the silence of the shadows
is not a place to live
sleep in a golden halo
and bathe in the light

i used to be a dreamer
the fog rolled through during adolescence
achingly cold and freezing me
the sun hasn't returned
to burn the fog away
my vision remains clouded
how can i heal
when i cannot see?

and some nights
i find it hard to sleep
to find peace
wedged between my conscience
and my soul

i am 2am thoughts
whispers in the night
the way rain falls silently.
the pink clouds of a sunset
morning dew as it settles on the grass.
i am unrequited love
wild flowers
soft guitar chords.
i am here;
i am everywhere

maybe love isn't meant to stay all night. it sits in the silence between laughter around the fire. it sways in the soft breeze of summer in the park, drinking flat lemonade and warm sausages in cheap white bread. it lingers behind the green eyes who can't find the words. love stays where love is meant to, in the lounge room of your childhood home and etched in the grooves of the dining room table. the stained wood who saw birthday after birthday, cold candle wax and stale crumbs. love seeps like warm honey into every crevice of your life, making a home where it chooses. and sometimes, that is a dark haired boy for one night or a soft grey cat for a few years not enough. love will stay, and you will be loved every day of your life. we just need to find it in the silence.

i scream
and i scream
and i scream
my body shakes
the earth rotates
and i wake up
again

i grieve
for the lost time
spent staring at walls
staring at nothing
years have gone by
i am still a child
for i never had the time
to grow
when everyone else was
i stared
at nothing
for years

sometimes i disappear
everything/everyone is just too
loud
maybe this time
i'll find myself
if i do not
at least i'll get some sleep
and rest in the silence

i became cold
not in the way that fresh snow
stings my skin
and stands the little golden hairs upright
i ran cold
in the way that i shudder at the fingertips
of my lovers
i cannot force myself to feel through a vast eternity
sometimes
if i let myself stray and think of you
it feels as if my lungs have frozen over
ice blooming in my throat
my blood slowing
until i catch my breath again
maybe that's what it means
to run cold

it runs through my fingers like honey
thick and syrupy at first
warming to my body heat
it turns to liquid
disappearing
and leaving me covered
with nothing to hold

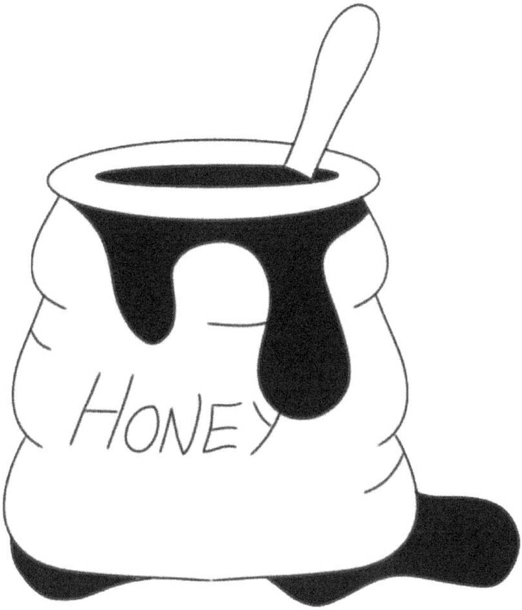
HONEY

sat in the gutter
i yawned
my eyes watering
glittering in the light
of the dim street lamp
you yawned too
cigarette stuck to your lip
smoke curling from your nose
i knew
we knew
this was the last time
we'd sit together
we were always so far apart

if this is enough
if this is what it feels like
i do not want it
i do not want
to be enough

the sun still rises
the rain still falls
i'll wake up
and you get to sleep
forever

i hope you are at peace

i will wade out
until my thighs burn
deep in an ocean of flowers
i will take the sun in my mouth
and leap into the thick air
eyes closed
and try not to choke

the thistles
in my heart
are being outgrown
by sunflowers

the biggest tragedy is
i was given soft, pale skin
and bright eyes
a gentle body holding a tormented soul

i guess i could be mad, that an unknown virus from an unknown country left me in my room for a year; stole a year of my twenties. i could cry, i could scream, i could mourn the loss. but i have been rotting in this room for years. the sickness just gave me permission.